Printed in Great Britain
by Amazon

53146318R00057